THE PROMISE OF WINTER

THE PROMISE OF WINTER

Quickening the Spirit
on Ordinary Days
and in Fallow Seasons

Martin Marty and Micah Marty

WILLIAM B. EERDMANS PUBLISHING COMPANY

GRAND RAPIDS, MICHIGAN / CAMBRIDGE, U.K.

THE PROMISE OF WINTER
Quickening the Spirit on Ordinary Days and in Fallow Seasons

Photographs copyright © Micah Marty.
✓ The FoundView checkmark assures the viewer that the key elements in these photographs were not moved, added, deleted (except by cropping), or significantly altered before or after the picture was taken.

Psalm quotations on pages 15, 19, 23, 27, 32, 52, 55, 56, 63, 67, 72, and 75 are from The New English Bible © 1961, 1970 the Delegates of the Oxford University Press and the Syndics of the Cambridge University Press. Psalm quotations on pages 24, 48, 60, 64, 76, 79, 88, and 102 are from Revised English Bible copyright © 1989 by Oxford University Press and Cambridge University Press. Psalm quotations on pages 39 and 47 are from Revised Standard Version Bible copyright 1952, 1971 Division of Christian Education of the National Council of the Churches of Christ in the United States of America. All other scripture quotations are from New Revised Standard Version Bible, copyright 1989 Division of Christian Education of the National Council of the Churches of Christ in the United States of America. Used by permission.

Cover design: Stephanie Hartings
Separations and printing: Gardner Lithograph, Buena Park, California
The Laser Fultone process is a registered trademark of Gardner Lithograph.

Library of Congress Cataloging-in-Publication Data

Marty, Martin E., 1928–
    The promise of winter : quickening the spirit on ordinary days and in fallow seasons /
Martin Marty and Micah Marty.
        p.   cm.
    ISBN 0-8028-4436-7 (pbk. : alk. paper)
    1. Bible. O.T. Psalms — Meditations. 2. Consolation — Meditations.
I. Marty, Micah, 1960–   . II. Title.
BS1430.4.M17   1997
242 — dc21   97-16698
                                                         CIP

Manufactured in the U.S.A.

01   00   99   98   97   9   8   7   6   5   4   3   2   1

To the memory of Joseph Cardinal Bernardin

. . . who taught us how to "let go" in life

as well as how to "hold on" to the promise of God

. . . and who found the psalms to be

"very special because they relate in a very direct, human way

the joys and sorrows of life, the virtues, the sins."

(The Gift of Peace)

Author's Introduction

Is the promise of winter spring? Not in this book. Here we use the image of winter to describe a condition of our hearts on ordinary days in every season. Here *winter* refers to the quiet times, the occasions when we lean back to search our interior lives. It represents some of the "down" sides that come every ordinary day—disappointments, setbacks, frustrations, puzzlements, and even temptations to doubt and depression and despair. To employ spring as the metaphor for whatever improves that condition would be to suggest that winter itself has no promise. Yet it does.

While we may choose to live where the winter climate never brings storms or to leave northern places during the most severe seasons, we will not successfully avoid winter in the soul. Better then to find the resources to cope with such a season of the heart than to evade it and wait for the solution imaged by "spring."

Winter has its inevitable place in the human condition. Farmers know that in the rhythm of the year and the nature of the soil, there is a reason for fields to lie fallow for a season—winter. So too we know that in the rhythm of the day and the nature of the soul, there are reasons for the pace of our thought and for our spiritual reflections to vary.

Promise, in this book, refers to God and what God offers in the quiet times and for the interior life. The promise comes from what we hear as the word of God. It represents here and now, for this day and this moment, a sense of the Presence to be realized each day, each night, with no waiting for spring. (In our tradition *promise = gospel,* the promise of God equals the activity of a God whose steadfast love speaks to and through Israel and definitively through the sacrificial love of Jesus Christ. And *promise = pro + missio,* which means being sent out to walk in the ways of God.)

In an earlier book, *A Cry of Absence,* I drew upon the psalms to address the winter of the heart. In these pages we also draw on that same biblical source, which believers have found helpful and fulfilling for thousands of years. Today much spiritual writing makes it seem as if life can be all simple joy and ecstasy, that authors in the religious field should guarantee that readers will smile and be sunny, and instinctively and instantly come up with praise-the-Lords. The biblical psalm writers do not make such claims. They carry us into the depths and through them. The psalmists do not cheat and offer evasions or easy solutions. Realism colors all that they say and sing.

In the pages that follow, we will listen to that realism as we live the ordinary days and fallow seasons of our life. Reasserting the promises of God in the midst of our winter and strengthened by them, we will find that our days, though they may not turn to spring, will indeed be different.

Martin E. Marty

Photographer's Introduction

I s the beauty of winter like that of a picturesque postcard? Is it like a Currier-and-Ives print of high-stepping horses drawing sleighs of revelers through snow-blanketed landscapes? Not in this book. Most of us know that winter—and life—are seldom so carefree, so sugarcoated.

Winter's other, less superficial beauty—the subject of this book—is harder to appreciate and more difficult to face but ultimately, we contend, more valuable. This more durable form of winter beauty involves not so much what winter *looks like* but what it *does*, to our environment and thus to us. The experience of winter—and not merely its appearance—is the subject of the photographs.

The photographs (and words) are not descriptions of specific places but rather metaphors for some of the universal aspects of winter (and wintry spirituality). Thus as you read and ponder what wintry spirituality does to the human landscape, it may be helpful to consider how the images in this book represent what winter does to the natural landscape.

Winter *clarifies*. Between the bright light, the clear air, and the absence of obscuring foliage on the trees, winter lets us see farther and more clearly. We may not always like what we see—particularly after the magical snow has melted and we face a bleak and barren landscape—but at least winter lets us more clearly see what we are up against.

Similarly, winter *reveals*. Winter strips away the ephemeral. The tree, unfettered by foliage and streamlined against the winter winds, looks both more vulnerable and more steadfast than it does when it sways with summer breezes.

But winter also *covers*. Even the roughest thickets of thorns and brambles are covered by smooth undulations of snow. Forest ways that are impassable in the summer become almost inviting under a smooth snowy blanket. Yet the drifts cover much beauty as well—the flowers and leaves and animals that in warmer months provide constant reminders of life.

Finally, winter *strengthens*. Thus this book (and these pictures) are not just about survival, of "making it through the winter," but about the transforming and strengthening nature of the winter experience.

Winter can be difficult, challenging, and uncomfortable, but it does make us stronger—and therein lies its beauty.

Micah Marty

Notes about the photographs can be found on pages 107–109.

One Day, One Page,
One Psalm, One Promise

If you page through *A Promise of Winter* as you would any book of pictures, we hope that you will find the images of winter on the farm and in the city, in woods and wilderness, near stream and field, intrinsically alluring. Perhaps you will enjoy the photographs for the way they capture remembered winters or will follow the way an artist's eye helps you see what you might have overlooked.

We also hope that the meditations—each of which focuses on one promise for the winter of the heart—will inspire reflections of your own. Some meditations may match your mood or meet your need for the moment. Others you may wish to store away mentally for the day when the promise, named in the meditation title, will speak most directly to you. (Read each title as if it is preceded by "The promise of.") Like other relatively short books, this one invites the reader to take it whole, perhaps in a single evening or during a long flight.

Yet another use of the book, that of "one day, one page," has proved to be the most popular among readers of our first two books of reflections and photographs, *Places Along the Way* and *Our Hope for Years to Come.* Since these pages are designed for your use on ordinary days and in fallow seasons, we think that they can address some aspect of your situation and spirit every single day and thus can be used in the sequence presented here. Perhaps each morning you will read the short Bible verse above the reflection and take in the facing picture. After reading the meditation, you might memorize the prayer, keeping it and the picture in mind throughout the rest of the day. Some may choose to take this opportunity to make a broader, deeper use of Scripture by reading the psalm along with the suggested text from elsewhere in Scripture that matches the spirit of the meditation and picture for that day. In some cases we have used the same psalm text more than once but in different translations, each of which was selected for language and images particularly appropriate when meditating on the winter of the heart.

Perhaps you will read the meditation and study the picture at the end of the day, using both to assess your inner life for the day past, seeking quiet rest, and hoping for resolve for tomorrow. Some have used the photo-text pairings in our previous books during "hymn-sings" (this time it would be "psalm-sings") and in adult classes and prayer groups. Others have said that they are not part of a believing community but still find personal ways to let these combinations work on them and for them.

These forty-seven pairings of photographs and text are ideal for use during Lent. If you begin reading a promise a day on Ash Wednesday, you will find the book climaxes on Easter. Yet however you choose to read this book, you will, we hope, find yourself on a pilgrimage, a pilgrimage we take with you, guided by the promises of the God of all seasons.

Newness

Psalm 51:10–12
Create in me a clean heart, O God,
and put a new and right spirit within me.

From heart*ache* and heart*break,* through heart*heaviness* and heart*less* and then on to heart*sick,* the dictionary offers an alphabetic review of what it means to be dispirited. If we pause for a moment to uncover the place of such words in our memories, disturbing events or expressions of low moods will come to mind to match each of them.

From ancient times until this day, people have used the word *heart* to refer to the depths of life from which or to which everything points or flows. We ask others to "have a heart" or to tell what is in their "heart of hearts." They are to go at something "heart and soul" or to "put their heart into" whatever they are doing.

The broken heart, which cannot repair itself, cries for help. A psalm singer, refreshed by the promises of God, asks for each of us that God would "create a clean heart within me," knowing that the old heart is soiled. "Wash me," the prayer adds, "and I shall be whiter than snow."

In climates where winter is warm, citizens welcome rains that rinse away accumulated litter and scum. Where fallen snow signals the depth of winter, those who walk in it revel in the awareness that its crystal beauty covers the grime and the gray. Never content merely to experience a superficial washing and an unlasting cover, the heart of the believer, revisiting the ancient promise, also asks for a "right spirit," the kind of spirit that produces nothing but newness within — now.

Not able to achieve a whole heart alone, I plead for help;
not able to right my own spirit, I ask for your gift of newness
and rightness. Amen

Romans 6:3–11

Security

Psalm 27:1–5
He will raise me beyond reach of distress.

After snow has fallen, anyone who is pursued grows freshly alert. The escapee from a prison camp knows that guards will track him best in new snow. Those who chase will find the one fleeing easy to follow. No hounded animal would seek more frantically than he for a place to hide beyond harm's way, whether in sun or shadow.

The running refugee yearns for slight drifts to cover the trails and traces he has left: "If only I had a lookout, a vantage from where I could see but not be seen. Yes, for a place to crouch unnoticed, so I could be free to observe. The pursuer would then tire or grow confused and leave me alone." That kind of dream is realized whenever a divine hand leads, whenever a loving guide provides a hiding place. Such a dream does not have to be a mere fevered fancy gone astray.

Serious persons need invest little imagination to see themselves not pursued but chilled by fear of forces or persons who will not let them come to and ever after enjoy secure places. Fears plague us daily, whether we are apparently succeeding or failing. Feeling assailed, we run away. But the experience of being moved beyond danger by God offers a new and daily ever more secure situation of safety and perspective.

Let me be moved to where I can gain a vantage on what is threatening; provide security while I elude the soul's assailants. Amen

Hebrews 6:13–15

Horizons

Psalm 55:6–8
O that I had wings like a dove!
I would fly away and be at rest.

Always humans reach and dream ahead. Lovers of colored leaves yearn for autumn to arrive. In fall, skiers crave snowy winters, whereupon shiverers long for spring. Spatially, pioneers move to frontiers, and all sorts of people envision horizons beyond which they could adventure, there to soar as if with gulls or to float in the air with doves. Outreaching these harmless fantasizings about what is next, what is beyond, are realistic hopes that they, that we, could move beyond what now holds us back and thereafter find new places spiritually to rest and reside.

The biblical writer who voiced the wish for wings was seeking a shelter "from the raging wind and tempest" of life as well as from circumstances gone wrong. He has a successor here and now—in this room, or under this sky— in each of us. Just beyond the edges of routine life on any day there lurks some threat that prompts a yearning for escape. Such threats menace calendars and agendas. They become hazards just when we need to think clearly, to focus. And thinking clearly means pondering the promises.

Thereupon not the image of an elegant dove but instead a stronger figure inspires a longing that is never misguided or misguiding. This One beckons beyond horizons, in the paths of Jesus Christ, who promises first adventure and then rest. We are free to follow.

Sustain me, Lord, so that the flight I long for
will not be a vain escape but a realistic movement
toward the repose you promise. Amen

Hebrews 11:8–10

Radiance

Psalm 59:9–10, 14–17
O my strength,
to thee I turn in the night-watches.

The traveler, tired as he is, abandons his trudging way and quickens his pace as darkness comes. Another, awakened early, greets the morning sun through half-refreshed eyes, eager as she is to leave miles behind, before the dark that is only hours ahead will arrive. Military lookouts, bored though they have been under the sunlit canopy of the day, know the hours around midnight as bringers of ennui and terror alike. In those hours, insomniacs turn and toss, counting minutes while unwillingly rehearsing in their disquieted minds the half-finished events of yesterday and dreading the half-fulfilling bids of tomorrow.

In the dark, one is weak and, desiring strength, turns to the light. What matters, what makes all the difference, is the turning. From darkness to light, from floundering to finding, from pointless wandering to discovering direction, from restless churning to purposeful activity—these are the promised moves. We realize them now in confidence.

This confidence comes not from a self-lit inner glow but from the lasting light that shines from outside ourselves. Such dawning comes with the radiance of God's sun and God's Son. This brightness shines invitingly when other lights and comforts, strengths and reliances, have disappeared. Dark surrounds, but this light is renewed whenever in crisis or custom, as at this moment, we rely on God to be ally and guide.

If you light and enlighten my ways and days,
I fear no boredom, no nights,
for you have shone and are shining into my heart. Amen

John 1:1–5

Praise

Psalm 148
Praise the Lord . . . snow and frost,
stormy wind fulfilling his command!

No doubt as if by instinct we picture in our minds, as artists do on canvas, that it is always springtime in the garden called Eden. No equator severs it, and perspiration never falls there. No leaf has dropped in it. Certainly, in this imagining, no glacier glides, no avalanche rumbles, no opal-crusted snow or crystalline icicles form.

Winter, says the mind whose eye does such picturing, belongs to the aftermath of Eden. Those who have lost fingers to gangrene after having been rescued from a blizzard or those who stomp to keep their circulation going at a bus stop curse the season. It is natural to envision that it was after paradise had been lost that winter was invented. In the old story, seeds were in the original gift and promise, but seedtime and harvesttime were not followed by a fallow season.

If such pictures dominate, winter needs re-presentation. Not only recreational skiers and sledders find a cherished place for the season. Cities below mountains fill their reservoirs and stay alive thanks to the snows above that shed their melting waters downslope. Horticulturists and farmers are eloquent about the need for fallow times after seeding.

Why not celebrate all this? Prose will not do; let there be psalms. If, as the story says, celestial creatures sang and sing to celebrate creation, now encourage terrestrial snow and frost to do so also.

When the extravagant sounds of nature discomfort me,
grant me ears properly to hear; when they seem silent,
give me a voice for praise. Amen

Isaiah 55:6–13

A i d

Psalm 18:1–6
Destructive torrents overtook me . . . ;
then in anguish of heart I cried to the Lord.

The "when" of prayer has much to do with the "what" and "how" of praying. Temporary escapees from winter cold or residents where it is always clear can feel calm when they look out the window at the palm trees. In the north, on the morning after snow, the view of the sun through the frost-laced window pleases. The breakfaster who gazes out feels at home in the world. Praise, not a desperate cry, is then the natural voice.

Let the hurricane bend the palms on another day or let snow thawed into streams send foreboding floods toward homes and people will experience a different situation of "when." A few mortals never have to experience dire weather situations and can only imagine them. But no mortals go through life without having to deal with figurative torrents or avalanches of adversity in their hearts and souls.

The CAT scan reports on cells gone wrong. A loved one suffers Alzheimer's disease and forgets to remember. Most suffering is quiet, so it comes in less vivid torrents. Recallings of a dead loved one, though often unbidden, bring stabs to the spirit. Or a job turns insecure, as does a once apparently serene marital relationship. One takes consequent actions, but first in all such storms we are bidden to cry out, to give voice to fears. Not showing cowardice but creative dependence, we who cry know that God the hearer welcomes our voices—and begins to help.

Give me a gift for praise, so that I will enjoy
a relationship that readies me for the cry for help
when it must come, perhaps today. Amen

Mark 4:35–41

Ecstasy

Psalm 5:1–8
Through your great love I . . . bow down in awe.

Awe rises in those who ponder the wonders of winter. In the face of a frozen waterfall or icily arrested billows, we gasp. Spontaneously we sputter to describe the glistening of ice in the dawn sun. Or in awe that feels like true fear we wonder at the power of storms in places of warm winters. No one apologizes for such responses to nature.

Along with awe comes ecstasy, as in the protected outdoors where parents play with children; in the clinic when the newborn glides from between a mother's thighs; when a startling dawn breaks. We enjoy—we do not explain anything— as awe and ecstasy combine.

Well and good. But what of awe in the face of the Lord of love or in the "holy temple"? In our day, some are critical: the notion of bowing before God could look like an act of enslaving submission. "How can one have self-esteem, dignity, and freedom when expressing awe?" they ask. But if they understand awe before God, who is the Other, the critics might well take a second look, own a second thought.

Philosopher Jerome Miller is helpful here as he ministers to our day's needs: The Other, the Sacred, "is that which, having been encountered, must be loved," because "the heart cannot do anything sensible, under its impact, except freely surrender itself."; the awed heart "no longer takes its desires seriously enough to mourn their loss" as ecstasy begins.

Let me hold back nothing today when I respond to love, however weakly, for my need is great and I welcome new desires. Amen

Ephesians 3:14–21

Carefreeness

Psalm 55:1–5
For my cares give me no peace.

Descendants of dwellers who lived on one island or another in a string of them tell stories of ancestors who traveled in winter across ice, from bit of land to bit of land. Some stories describe heroic mail carriers or physicians who made the winter rounds on sled or on foot in places where in other seasons boats would more safely have transported them.

Always these narratives are tinged by recall of dangers. Never could such travelers be at ease. They would set out carefree under sun and in hours find themselves full of care in a scene aswirl with blinding snow. They would fix their eye on storms in one direction and find them blowing in from another. They would be alert about coming too close to the edge of the ice, where death by drowning awaited them, only to risk losing sight of the distant island that had been their goal. If they never reached such a goal—a cottage with a lamp burning and a fire glowing—no one would hear the details of their end. If they did reach the destination, their grandchildren would never stop hearing of the hazards.

Such travelers, chronically full of care and, on occasion, acutely aware of danger, are our representatives on the stage of daily life. The possibility of the loss of direction, regular disappointments, and the disappearance of goals are our hazards. But in each case, the light of God assuredly shines through every storm and pulls us homeward.

> *In the confusions and storms that surround my neighbors and me, keep us in sight of our goal; protect us on a more carefree way. Amen*

Exodus 13:21–22

Safety

Psalm 4:3–8
For you alone, O Lord, make me lie down in safety.

The wintry sort of hazards that belong to the snow-filled wilderness or the heart in solitude find their match in the winter of the city and the heart in the crowd. Attend a funeral in the inner city of a large metropolis ("inner city" here being a code word for the poor, jammed, and often dangerous parts of town). You are likely to hear the preacher picture the wonders of the life to come in the place the deceased now enjoys. As often as not, heaven gets described as a site where no one needs locks on the door, fences topped with razor wire, or refuge from arsonists. In northern cities you will hear how the fear of fire in firetraps on subzero nights inspires the speaker to envision at last a warm, safe, permanent future place for innocents.

Praying a psalm prayer will not assure physical safety or offer fire prevention when icy air surrounds. But consistently praying every psalm, including the affirmation about the Lord alone that is on our minds at this moment, extends the visions of personal safety into the realm of the heart and spirit. There the fears that never want to leave us find their haunting house. We find reason to know repose while reflecting on the will and way of one who has "put gladness in my heart" through the activity of Jesus, who freed and frees. It was he who said—who says—"Fear not," and provides strength.

When this day ends, let me lie down in safety, warmed by the gladness that you have already put in my heart, and grant me peace. Amen

John 14:25–27

Purity

Psalm 51:1–9
Wash me, and I shall be whiter than snow.

In the world of the spirit, the plaguing alternative to clarity and purity is not black against white but gray against everything else. The soul, like the weather, can be grimy, dingy, cheerless. The wintry day and the human spirit alike turn gray, as does week-old snow in the city of traffic. Gray is an achromatic color; it has no hue. Admirable in some contexts—there can be much right about a gray dress—in other contexts our eyes pass gray on the way to both pastels and bright primary tones, tints that one might say have "made up their minds" and speak to us.

We might awaken any day to grayness without, grayness within. At any otherwise bright moment, the unwelcome shadow of the spirit that lacks hue can haunt people of any temperament and outlook. Grayness: people experience it not when they have finished something truly horrible but when they have left unfinished their intentions to do moderate good. A look into the mirror of the soul then reveals no color contrasts and the slate is stained. No self-help actions change that.

Ancients, to get rid of gray, used the bleach of the sun or worked with detergents and sulphur fumes. Followers of Jesus saw and see his gift of himself as the cleaner of the stained slate of lives. Believers in all ages know that God is the cleansing agent who creates the pure garment "whiter than snow" and the literally fresh slate for this day, this night.

> *Cleanse the grayness from the garment of my life, and let me face the day and the night with a sense of freshness and resolve. Amen*

Titus 2:11–14

Quiet

Psalm 83
O God, be neither silent nor still.

All is still now. Dwellers in snow country remark how after winter thunder and a blowing storm, silence can pall the snowscape. Poets call this preternatural, because it seems to exist eerily beyond nature. No bird song, no whistle of the wind, no crackle of a twig interrupts the quiet. Plants are at rest, as are households. Often that means all is well. Souls seeking escape from the tumult of business and busy people welcome such hours and occasions.

Such welcoming is for special times, however, because usually we need a sense that someone is near, that events can occur. The search for company is strongest when we feel danger or fear being isolated. When people long ago feared the stalking of their enemies, they cried to God to break the silence. So do people now; so it is with us now.

Whole seasons bring, with their coming, disappointments or depressions that can lead to the feeling that we are abandoned. When we most crave the direct voice of God, it seems most difficult to hear. When we most desire company, we feel most alone. Stillness at such times does not produce quiet within. Instead it awakens the kind of trauma that will be best interrupted by a cry: "O God!" Cultivating the presence of God today and listening helps assure that the only silences we experience are of the welcome sort: those that produce quiet in the fragile heart.

When you seem long absent from my disturbed heart, provide me with a sign of your presence, giving me the quiet and peace I seek. Amen

1 Kings 19:9–13

Worship

Psalm 84:1–2, 10–12
My soul longs, indeed it faints
for the courts of the Lord.

Fainting with desire to be somewhere else is usually a notion associated with daydreamers, the fickle, spotters of celebrity, and searchers for sensation. To be present in the ballpark for the championship game though tickets are scarce; to be numbered with the groupies at a rock concert when the gates get closed; to want to see the miles disappear so that the beloved can be near— these are the occasions for virtual fainting that are comprehensible to millions in our time.

The idea of longing to be in the courts of the Lord seemingly would belong to another time or place. Pilgrims sang when they reached the lovely dwelling places of God, having along the way envied the nest-owning swallows and sparrows and dreamed of the lovely dwelling places of God. While grand cathedrals and architectural gems invite many travelers on the spiritual way to come from windswept, snowdrifted paths into safe and beautiful settings, most of the time we make our pilgrimages on practical paths leading to markets or work.

One realizes that what made the Temple, the courts, and the dwelling places of God attractive were not the candelabra, the hangings, or the fall of light on congregations. What lured and lures, what mattered and matters in the humblest of settings, is the presence of the One whose courts they are, who satisfies our longings now and here.

> *Satisfy me with your presence in your portable precincts, the figurative courts and settings where you are literally available. Amen*

Matthew 18:20

Rescue

Psalm 69:1–5, 13–18
I have come into deep waters,
and the flood sweeps over me.

I am in this over my head!" Not "We are in this over our heads!" A venture-
some person, diving alone, has taken a dare. Thereupon he is swept along by
currents too strong. Or a bad risk beguiles an investor who plunges. She is
overwhelmed. An owner loves possessions too much and too long. Clinging to
them, he notices too late the still chill flood from winter's thaw that takes all
with it and carries him into caverns and crevasses of horror. "I am in this over
my head!"

Pictures of floods in rage and of desperate victims as they come up for one last
gasp evoke recallings of times when we felt spiritually powerless, swept by the
furies, out of reach, alone. Seldom does a season or even a day pass that does
not lead most of us to a confusion that can be voiced in the phrase of panic:
"I am in this over my head!" Such a realization can be the first step toward
help. Often it has not been.

Why? The searcher of her heart recognizes that on any day, maybe this day,
memories of wrongs done and stabbings of guilt can paralyze: "O God, you
know my folly; the wrongs I have done are not hidden from you." Yet her cry
need not be the last word. The crier, in danger of being swept along, remembers the one hand that reaches, and responds: "In the abundance of your
steadfast love, answer me. . . . rescue me . . . from the deep waters." That
love still reaches, grasps, and holds.

When I am "in over my head," you know my need, O Lord;
give me a heart and voice to pray and the promise to hear. Amen

Matthew 14:23–33

Fearlessness

Psalm 23
Even though I walk through the valley of the shadow of death, I fear no evil.

At the end of the valley of the shadow of death are death itself and then graveyard, so often visited in mind. Dwelling on that end thought can destroy a day. Being mortal is one thing; being morbid is another. Letting autumn signal the death of leaves is one thing; letting winter have the last word is another. Walking through the valley of the shadow of death is one thing; fear of evil is another.

Whether rising on the brightest day or ending one when illness and sorrow shade the dark hours, people of faith cherish as much as any remembered phrase these favorite words that help them walk wherever. As through a valley? Beasts and robbers threatened those in ravines. Explore a canyon until darkness falls while winter storms surprise and you will know why ancients feared such places. Our fears are directed less to *death*—believers who are long in pain often welcome it—but to the *shadow* of death that dogs us daily. Fear comes. But then one affirms:

"For thou art with me." Most believers have this verse so regularly in mind that they might not have taken it to heart, where it belongs. "You are with me" is a very personal line about a personal presence. The Shepherd who guides and cares, who offers the warmth and safety of the plain in springtime, is available and wants to be bidden, "You are with me," to guide through the spiritual winter.

Remove the great shadow across this life—the fear of death—giving me confidence in your presence this day and night. Amen

John 10:11–16

Worth

Psalm 8
*What are human beings that you are mindful of them,
mortals that you care for them?*

Pit a climber against a Himalayan peak where perpetual winter reigns, take a picture, and study it to get a sense of proportion. Against the swirl of winds on peaks, half-lost in clouds, roped against cliffs, overleaping crevasses, a single dangling and apparently insignificant human figure, barely discernible, looks pitiful, worthless.

Even up close on flat land, the winter scene changes the perspectives with which we measure. Frontier farmers told of strong pioneers who bucked the blizzards but, weakened, were lost between farmhouse and barn, to wander and die, unnoticed until sere spring.

The human, a speck against the peaks or on the plains, also looks trivial during her brief moment in the crowd. The language of faith, however, pictures God seeing humans as creatures of immeasurable worth. The One who made each of us is mindful, is a rememberer, aware of us even when others lose us in that crowd. *That* God remembers is itself a great claim. But the greater wonder comes with an awareness of *how* we are remembered. Words from long ago still ring true: the One whose fingers made the heavens and the stars *cares* for each. In the loving care of a dying and risen Christ, those named in his name realize that they are now ready to be lost in the crowd but never truly lost: found in him.

*Lost by others, often even missing to myself, let me today be found
mindful of your mindfulness, careful in responding to your care. Amen*

Matthew 10:28–31

Shelter

Psalm 27:5–14
He will hide me in his shelter in the day of trouble.

Not all times are times of trouble, but no day passes without the fear of troubling misfortunes crossing our mind, there to threaten our heart and paralyze actions. At the day's work, we may experience tensions piling up to the point that relations with others break. A crisis of health, an anxious decision, an apparent dead end in family living—we remember facing these or fear the need to do so now or in the future. Old funeral prayers thanked God for leading the deceased through "this troublous life," the adjective being apt for most people.

The "days of trouble" can arrive subtly, like a mist that confuses, or suddenly, like a snow squall that surprises journeyers; always unsought, distress will come. Just as often, we strugglers simply lose our pathways. If only we could make it through this night, this day. If only there were refuge, where we could be safe and could recover resources.

Those caught off guard on forbidding and treacherous trails find relief when their distressed company comes across a cave, a hollow, or, best of all, a shelter. Only one, God, reliably is there. Stumbling upon this sanctuary we discover that, long and usually overlooked, it has been available all along. The Provider of that shelter waits to rescue us as we stumble. The provision of shelter offered so freely is a strength and security for this day and brings the richness of promise for tomorrow.

With all my heart I seek the shelter your presence and word provide;
help me to find again the map and the path to you for this day. Amen

Isaiah 4:2–6

Escape

Psalm 55:4–8
I would flee far away;
I would lodge in the wilderness.

The heroic self-made person would defy all misfortune. Let bankruptcy happen and he would recover his reliable name. Let illness threaten and she would think the right thoughts and eat the right organic foods and thus keep disease at bay. Such strivers would set the terms for conquest.

Then this person looks in the mirror and sees, beyond the image of bravado, a pair of frightened eyes, a worried look, a brow creased, a posture of cringing. None of us *are* masters of our souls and destiny. Circumstances will eventually defeat the strongest among us. Eager to change them, we might run from the complexities of life and from our situation in the crowded world to a place apart. The call would be to follow the Jeremiahs of prophecy: find the wilderness.

Romantic as that severe notion might sound on a summer's day, its lure disappears when winter comes into that sometime beckoning scene. The Siberias of the soul numb the extremities of spirit; the winds of desolation howl in the snow-furrowed recesses where the mind and heart take momentary refuge. Yet God is present also in the wilderness. There Jesus went to prevail against the tempting one. To such wastes the eccentric saints fled the world to find the call and hear the voice of God. Our own wildernesses are portable. The divine refuge is full of promise and will be wherever we go, refreshing, not withering, our spirits.

Let the lure of the wilderness and the escape it offers be turned into
the beckoning of refuge in the midst of my busy world this day. Amen

Luke 12:5–16

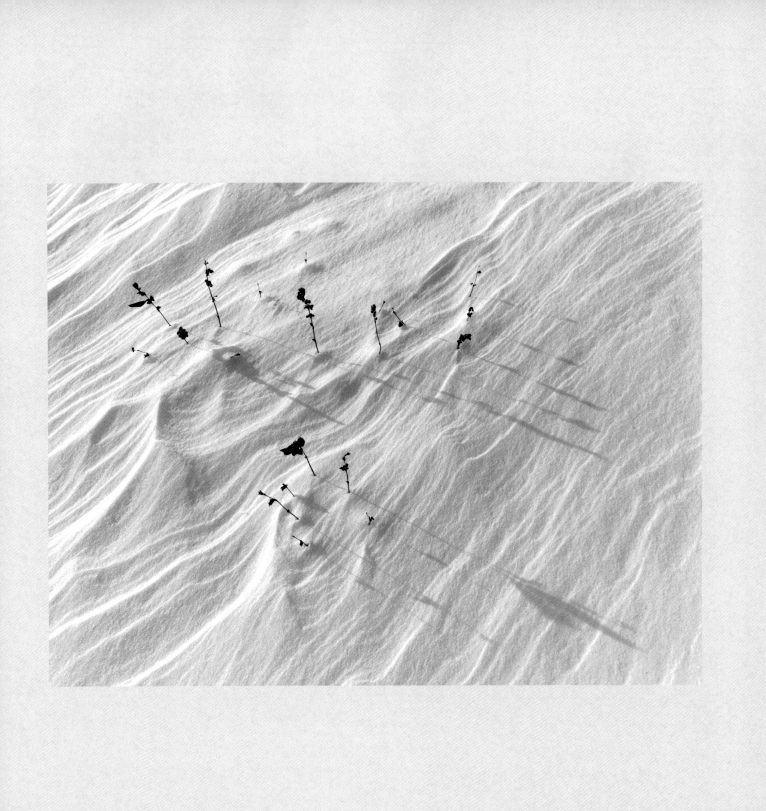

Expectancy

Psalm 25
For thee I wait all the day long.

Cellular phones and other devices permitting winter car-travelers to call upon potential rescuers have indeed aided saviors of the lives of those trapped in blizzard drifts. But the devices are also hazards. Their owners take greater risks than they would have before, thinking that being in contact means being rescuable.

Waiting, trapped travelers tell us later, they had huddled on their car seats, through seemingly endless nights and days of stupor. Stewarding food bits and batteries, some hallucinate. Those who keep their sanity sound like returned prisoners of war, Gulag survivors, the shipwrecked: they keep a most alluring image in mind and take direction from reconceiving it. Almost always they conjure one dream that becomes reality. If only I can again see the light in the window and the open door of beckoning home and house! If only I can be greeted by those most important to me as I rush up to them! To wait, and to wait more, is frustrating, boring, enraging. The only and worse alternative is *not* to wait. When the waiting is rewarded, life reacquires meaning.

We who have experienced absence and aloneness, who have suffered pain or disappointment—has anyone been exempt from these?—keep relearning: we are being waited for by the God who never tires, who is near, is here. And we grow through expectancy, in confidence.

> *As nights pass too slowly and days make their demands, visit me in your mercy with your mercies, and satisfy my longing at day's end. Amen*

Isaiah 30:15–18

Play

Psalm 119:169–176
Let the music of your promises be on my tongue.

Perhaps only in German romantic poetry about winter-day hikes in the Harz mountains do wanderers sing, sometimes with a little help from Johannes Brahms. Most of us merely shiver or, while climbing, work up a sweat but become too breathless to do tra-la-las. The clear air of a winter's day that makes the noise of jet airplanes sound so near lofts well the rare bird song or the shouts of snowball-throwing children in the park. Otherwise, silence. We usually save for summer picnic days our own outdoor songs and games. So it is with summer in the soul: voices then and there erupt readily into song or appreciate it. Not in winter.

There is no point in being literal about the condition of winter in the soul. It occurs whenever the tongue is heavy, the jaws are clenched, and the impulse to play is stifled. Even then, especially then, there is reason to cling to the promises of God and, perhaps in the quiet chambers of the heart, to sing of them. For we now realize that these promises come in any sort of weather and do not depend upon the approach of spiritual springtime. Now in the cold and silence when fields are fallow, we find special reason to listen for the promises. The Creator, the Redeemer, the Spirit of comfort assure us that we will never be comfortless. The good news in all seasons is that God is ahead of us and the divine ways are partly realized already, even before autumnal abundance is ours.

If I am stunned by silences, lost in the cold, let my reflection
on your promise lead me to "think" a song or a game
—or to sing and play. Amen

Isaiah 42:5–12

R o o m

Psalm 4
You gave me room when I was in distress.

Vaguely on some days and vividly on others, a special form of distress stalks the soul. Experts now borrow the German word *Angst* to express the deadening sense of limits. They connect it with the Latin word *angustiae,* a "narrows" in the landscape around, in the soul within.

German and Latin lessons only provide names for trauma, not help. Being practical people, we can free ourselves from some external threats. But from within come lasting assaults. Thoughts nag: We will die, and we know it. Things are not right with God and others. We lack the will to make them so. This place we know will be taken by others and we will be forgotten. Cornered beasts have more chance to escape their traps than have we by ourselves to move beyond our narrow places.

The imagination of a life without options, without space for the spirit or room to breathe, can make a day pointless, turn night into horror, and leave us in a perpetual winter of gloom. Yet the narrows of distress is not our destined place. Through the generations, in all places and circumstances, believers have learned to pray "give me room," a cry for space, and then to thank the freedom-giving God: "You gave me room." We think of the vastness of the prairie winter spaces: they call to mind the reality that God the giver provides this for our souls. Such a thought opens a panoramic vision on this day filled with opportunity.

Help me find vistas instead of narrows, freedom instead of traps,
as I show confidence in your acceptance, joy in your options. Amen

2 Samuel 22:17–20

Stability

Psalm 26
When once my feet are planted on firm ground,
I will bless the Lord.

Swamp and slush and slippery spots conspire to deprive those who would cross them of places to plant their feet securely. The act of watching anyone try to regain footing in the softness, or to find balance after sliding begins, elicits chuckles when comics are acting. Watching anyone on the verge of sinking or falling in real life or, worse for us, *being* the one who is sliding toward disaster, evokes horror.

In a new day we are called to make our way beyond the swamps of relativism, wherein nothing is true or sure. The slush that here stands for lack of all definition—where is the curb and where the sewer when definition goes?—leads to stumbling and misfortune. Slippery spots—what image better depicts hazards on the path on which each walks?

After travail, however, some travelers do arrive on paths and reach ground that is secure, if still cold. Beyond the refreezing slush near the curb is the well-swept sidewalk that beckons one to walk in trust. Having guided us past the spots where it was easier to fall than to stand, God waits to offer dry and high places. There the sun has done its work, and there the Son has done his. Who journeys with this God and the Son in whom God's fullness dwells has found firm ground and is able to grow in independence and strength, moving toward the destinies the day brings. Feet are not merely planted there. They move, briskly.

Firm, dry ground where once I had been slipping off balance: that is the soul's request for the walk I undertake in the hours ahead. Amen

Isaiah 26:1–13

Endurance

Psalm 39
Man . . . is but a puff of wind,
he moves like a phantom.

Puff: this is the sound of air invisible as it passes from pursed lips on a cold day. Like a gust of dust or snow that disappears with the breeze made by an opening door, it creates no sign unless the breath is warm and the air is cold. Certainly, such a short burst leaves no mark.

Old scriptures and new experiences lead people to compare the comings and goings of puffs, phantoms, and shadows to the passing character, the transience of all life. Who remembers achievements of most days? Who will remember anything of this ordinary day? A political prisoner once kept his sanity by trying to recall some event from every day of his life. Most were gone from memory. So now is he. The products of his recall were puffs of wind, and he a virtual phantom.

Are any efforts, then, worthwhile, since all things pass, including the acts of taking note of them and the people to take those notes? Yes: "And now, Lord, what do I wait for? My hope is in thee." The One who created time created the fact that it also passes, that all passes. This One, therefore, must have cared about commands and promises. This same and only One must have provided, and certainly did provide, for creatures to find meaning in the day that is passing and to find hope for tomorrow. We step forward in such hope today and tomorrow. Gone is the phantom; here is the enduring child of God.

Now, Lord, I wait in hope, living in the present, accepting the day's challenges, confident in the promises you have made. Amen

Luke 12:22–31

Prophecy

Psalm 74
We cannot see what lies before us,
we have no prophet now.

Gone, out of sight and hearing now, are the goads and rewards of parents and teachers who once gave direction. Gone, much of the time and for many, are the images of leaders in state and church, who once served as prophets to model the moral life. Gone from view are the maps charting the "absolutes" that once helped people steer their life course.

Any day, any hour, a loss of direction can afflict persons at work in the office. In family affairs, perspective becomes elusive. Even in one's safe and lit room, disorientation plagues and paralyzes. We lack landmarks that can serve as the signposts to mark dangers. We seek beckoning shelters; they often seem to lie just beyond the range of sight or become confusing in the ample thickets of reality.

Once, it is remembered, the voice of prophets gave direction, and they walked paths others could follow. Now, it is said, our land lacks such prophets, and we are directionless, wandering. Our ears are empty. But in the midst of what is remembered and is said, we may not have looked and listened with the care demanded in the heart's winter.

One signpost does remain, discernible in the shape of a cross, the mark of loving and divine sacrifice. This is to be found in the heart, when the eye cannot see. And *the* prophet, Jesus, speaks from that cross, to give clarity and perspective and hope. Help is available, this hour.

When I lose perspective or direction, let me hear from you the word pointing me to one sure sign: the cross of forgiving love. Amen

John 20:24–31

Protection

Psalm 57
In the shadow of your wings I will take refuge,
until the destroying storms pass by.

God with wings? Greek and other mythologies knew such gods, but the unseen God of the Bible has wings only in metaphor. Yet they serve well in an indirect way, since sometimes in the Scriptures, God gets compared to a protective fowl who gathers the helpless young under her wings. Elsewhere God covers the beloved with tent and tabernacle, roof and cave. Through the ages, those who welcome refuge are glad to see themselves and God pictured thus, connected in various ways.

Ages pass, and again and again predictors envision that never again will believers, especially city sophisticates, appreciate rural and homey imagery. But in each age the envisioners are wrong. There is something primal and heart reaching in these picturings, as in the case of "the shadow of your wings." Some will say that this notion of finding shelter should be outgrown: we are supposed to be mighty enough to stand on our own feet. Strong men and women, it is argued, do not seek places to hide from storms. They stand up to the wintry furies. But here, too, the "some" who will say this may not have had their own eyes open or their hearts ready. We are trained progressively to seek divine protection, not because we are not to display weakness but because the storms of life grow ever stronger. Faith promises we will outlast them.

Help me make vivid again the picture of the protection you offer;
then, with your grace, help me realize such refuge in the storms. Amen

Hosea 14:5–9

Meeting

Psalm 59
My strength, I look to you.

Some translations of the psalms locate our looking most intensely in the night watches. We may and must seek at all times, but watching demands the most attentiveness during the long night. Ask the military sentinel, who sees company and variety only during the day. Better, ask the soldier who on assignment must sneak past such a sentinel, or the unjustly imprisoned victim who is seeking to escape in twilight.

During the day many walk and leave tracks on the trail or in the snow, so the one who sneaks or who would escape can find some security by knowing that his own footpaths will be lost among the many. At night the trail, if there is one, will show but one set of footprints. They could lead to one's discovery, capture, and possible death. So in fear one waits. After the night watches, when dawn brings traffic and stir, *then* there can be relative safety. Until then?

In most translations, those who pray this psalm do one thing: they look. None of their watching focuses on any *thing*. Things cannot rescue, cannot give peace or safety against the enemies of the soul or against the challenges to the spirit. The word inspires us still: all of the watching is directed to "you," the God who, according to promise, will meet us. The God who "in unfailing love, will go before me," adds the psalm as it speaks to the heart, as readily today as when it was written.

> *Meet me, O God of steadfast love; shorten the night of fear*
> *and provide a path with the assurance of your presence,*
> *care, and invitation. Amen*

Luke 6:12–16

Sanctuary

Psalm 55
Soon I should find a sanctuary from wind and storm.

The whole of Psalm 55 frames all the spiritual searches for safe places. Words like "cares," "no peace," "panic-stricken," "trouble," "anguish," "terrors," and "trembling" come in fast succession here. Such a listing of the disturbances that lead some to seek sanctuary could itself become so unsettling that it might drive others to take refuge from the text. They would then seek sanctuaries that had not seemed necessary before.

A second reading of those words about trauma, however, bids us to welcome the promise that comes amid them. The words themselves realistically match the daylong nightmares and the nightly terrors of the mind, now well described as the "wind and storm" within. The needs of the soul drive thoughtful people to find places of refuge where they might gather strength for new encounters against enemies of the spirit.

The sanctuary in a literal winter may be a literal lean-to, an abandoned house or barn, a hollow, any place to hide. Faith impels believers also to look for more permanent, more graceful housing where, in the company of others, the seeker finds nourishment. Inside, God's people are welcome, and there they welcome each other. Believers rightly consider their places of congregational gathering to be such places. There may be discomforts also within, but for the hour the wind and storm are kept at a distance. Warmed, we leave to reengage them.

> *Receive me, hide me, and then send me back refreshed*
> *to serve among the winds that never stop,*
> *the storms no one but you can control. Amen*

Ephesians 2:13–22

Presence

Psalm 88

I am numbered with those who go down to the abyss.

A friend may tell you that he has good reason for belonging to a congregation where nothing but positive thoughts get uttered and songs of cheer resound. All week long, he says, he is in a competitive jungle with plenty of "downs." His cherished moments before God compensate for all these. Certainly God would not want him to *be* down, even for a moment.

His impulses are natural, and the congregation of praise *is* graced with reasons for joy. But the joy erupts in the face of realism. How do we address the fact that in the journey of life there can be icy crevasses and gulfs into which one could fall, never to be heard from again? Rare are the souls that never experience the threat of the the dark pits or know surely how to avoid a fall into an abyss. Senders of letters enclosed in Christmas cards often speak of abandonments by spouse or child or that cancer cells were malignant and the search for hope must begin at the beginning again. Doubt, depression, despair encircle the sender's soul or gnaw at it from within. Everything swirls toward the abyss.

In such lives the complaint of unrelieved agony, as voiced in this psalm, wins its place, even if only for that moment when realism most matters. What stands out clearly in these words that one would normally wish to hurry past is this: even in the abyss — or even in the midst of fear known at its edges — there are reasons to call out to the God of promise.

64

Leave me never without a sense that I can reach you, that even in the depths of life you are there, to listen and offer promise and help. Amen

Isaiah 51:12–16

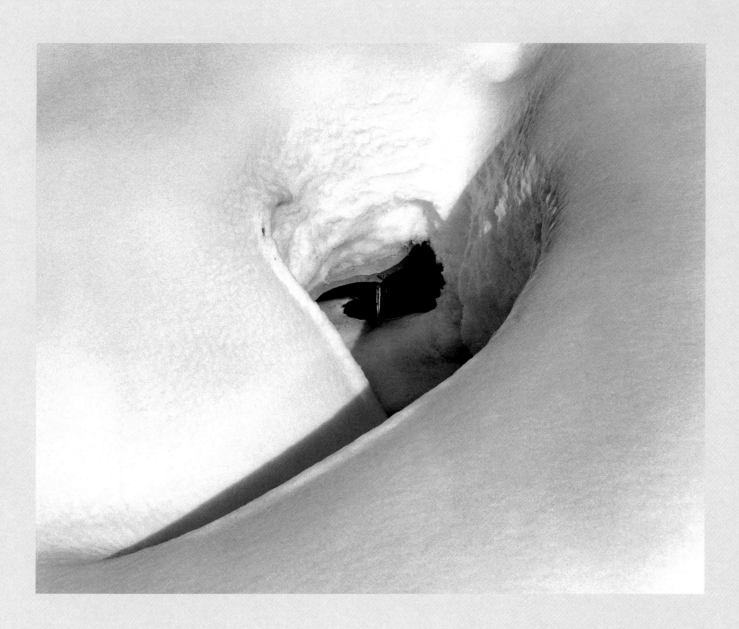

Refreshment

Psalm 63
I seek thee early with a heart that thirsts for thee.

Start the day with the news of the world or with a glance at an overcrowded agenda or calendar, as many or most of us do, and we find ourselves disoriented and full of anxieties. Where is God in all the world's suffering? Where am I going to find time and resource and energy to meet the challenges of the next twelve or eighteen hours?

Almost all spiritual directors urge that we develop a good habit, until what had been second nature at best now becomes first nature. They want us to learn to fill our thoughts at dawn with an awareness of the presence and care of God who has guarded our sleep. We are next to take an inventory of needs. But go deep as we might, there are to be found few resources for the soul to nurture itself, to produce refreshment.

Search, then, your inner adult or the inner child, suggests a different kind of counselor. So we look again: where in our own innerness will be found an assured flow of nourishment? Without the spring of waters from below or the flow of waters from upstream, what could be the source of renewal? We would remain barren, like unfed rivulets long obscured, leaving only parched beds of memories. Instead, God gives us freedom to draw on the stream of divine gifts that reach the thirsty tongues and throats of all of us who long for them, who awaken to what is being offered in every need that will face us during a day.

Longing for the water of life, I come to you, its very source, confident that I will not be left in dryness, but will live in strength. Amen

John 7:37–39

Wholeness

Psalm 34
*The Lord is near to the brokenhearted,
and saves the crushed in spirit.*

The durability of the human spirit surprises those who chronicle the travails of most lives. As for the body: a few too many hours of exposure to the frigid, the loss of blood circulation by a stumbler into the snowbank, the heart attack resulting from overexertion by the senior snow shoveler—these all can lead to loss of life. Yet on many occasions the well-ensouled body of a believer resists threats to the tested human spirit.

Despite some regular records of endurance, frequent and familiar are the accounts of the overburdened spirit being crushed. Parents can mourn inconsolably when an innocent bystanding son gets killed during gang shoot-outs. Patient and loving spouses find love denied, until they are pushed too far, and at least for a time become crushed. Or someone once trusted breaks faith and the trusting one experiences heartbreak.

Often the broken heart and the crushed spirit mean the end of particular stories. Not all recover. But the beginning of recovery, when it comes, occurs when the nearness of God is palpable. Believers identify with Jesus praying in a garden. They fear the divine abandonment that his cry from the cross seems to suggest. But they are believers because ever after his cry, they have come to know that God is not an abandoner but one who wants to be near. Cultivating that sense of nearness is an act that gives meaning to this day and to the spirit that does the cultivating.

> *Nearness, not distance; heart's healing, not brokenness;*
> *wholeness, not crushedness: for these I yearn;*
> *this I would experience. Amen*

Matthew 26:36–44

Provision

Psalm 5:11–12
Spread your protection over them,
so that those who love your name may exult in you.

An African diplomat early in life won a scholarship to study in the United States. Later he confessed that he had always known the *idea* of cold. But that meant nothing. College years in Minnesota instructed him about its reality. Out of necessity he learned to protect himself by adding layers of outer clothes. For a time he resisted embarrassing ear muffs. Yet eventually he welcomed even the silly-looking garment that, being close to his frail ears, gave him comfort and helped him survive. Through it all, he noticed that life went on. People went about their business, having planned for the cold and barren times to come.

The same God who promised that seedtime and harvest would never disappear from the earth gave people the brains to face the seasons. They learned to store up food against the threat of famine, to set aside fodder for their animals in the grassless seasons. In a way, they came to share in the providence, the providing, of God. And those among them who believed in God were privileged to acknowledge their source and to exult, while giving thanks and enjoying divine protection.

The promises of God can appear pointless to those who do not use the provided means for finding help that this God offers, as when in the gift of Jesus Christ more love than we need is made available.

> *Nurture my love for you, Divine Protector; motivate me*
> *to be provident in my response and to share with others. Amen*

1 Corinthians 12:4–26

Growth

Psalm 143
To thee I lift my outspread hands,
athirst for thee in a thirsty land.

*T*undra: the Russians gave us the word, perhaps because they had so much of the reality to share. The tundra is treeless, bushless, vast, and level. North of it, ice and snow agelessly refuse to recede. South of it, the ground may occasionally thaw. Here, in the in-between locale, one encounters a virtual desert of the northland, where brooks do not flow, lakes do not thrive, melted snow cannot nourish, and no one stands by to offer help.

The barren soul, the unnourished inner life, bears the marks of the tundra: spiritual starving threatens. Those who languish might envy and then wish to flee to the lush southlands, where waters do flow, hands are said to reach generously, and there are supposed to be ready smiles. But tundras are portable. Desertification or progressive ice covering afflicts that inner life of people in all physical climates and can take over among unalert believers, including us.

The first step in recovery, the first move toward nourishment, comes with an acknowledgment of need. This need impels a gesture, a reaching out and up, as it were, with weak hands, to be opened as for a gift. The gift has long been ready, offered as it is by the divine hand that has been reaching for us all along. From it come both the means to enrich our soul's environment and the warmth to let love grow.

> *In the vast desolations of the heart, create in me a quiet center;*
> *in the spiritually treeless and thirsty land,*
> *refresh me and help me grow. Amen*

Matthew 26:36–44

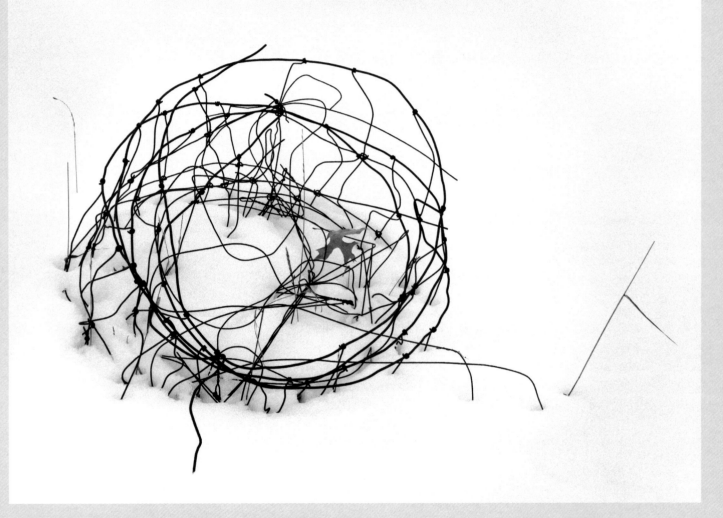

Audience

Psalm 77
In the day of my trouble I seek the Lord.

The long hours of the spiritually wintered night, when the chill of the air matches the cold in the heart, when the winds around replicate the storms within, are at once the most pressing and the most frustrating times for prayer. The beginning of this psalm suggests a prior connection between God and the one who prayed: "I cried aloud to God" and, of course, God "heard me." But as darkness came, everything changed: "All night long I was in deep distress, as I lay thinking, my spirit was sunk in despair." With the company of others gone, devastation came.

But do company and clarity always arrive with the day? Many of us wake up to face complicated living, entanglements with problems we cannot solve, apparently lifeless relations with those to whom we would reach in love and concern. Then the poet of this psalm asks for us: Has the divine love now failed us? Will the promises of God go unfulfilled? "Has God forgotten to be gracious," and has the divine right hand "lost its grasp" and let us go? Where is the divine compassion?

God and the graced believer who prays can become rewebbed. Confusions may surround, but within, the experience of the God who meshes divine purposes with our needs and will not let us go offers loving concern. It will remain with us until morning, in the morning, and through the long day's adventures and ordinary doings.

> *As my soul reaches, let me find that you reached first, entangling me in your love, readily being at work to fulfill your promises. Amen*

Isaiah 27:2–5

Dwelling

Psalm 84:2–9
*I pine and faint with longing
for the courts of the Lord's temple.*

Envy the sparrow, in its often aimless flight? Be jealous of the swallow whose swoops lead it only to sparse food? Envy other beings small and weak, just because they have homes and nests? Envying the birds, or at least pointing to their example, was precisely what seekers long ago would do. Far from the holy place which was their own true home, they yearned to be where the presence of God was announced. Anywhere else spelled homelessness and meant being adrift, lost.

In the winter of our days, physical warmth for most of us is only a twist of the thermostat dial away. Some versions of "the courts of the Lord's Temple" are as available as the offerings labeled "Churches" in the Yellow Pages. But in the winter of the heart, distraction keeps us from appreciating the holiness that could alter our lives, the warmth that is at hand in the company of gathered believers.

So it will be, until we recall the promise of the Presence, and then let it work on our imagination and experience. If we are away too long from the courts of the Lord, we may go off on aimless flights where no satisfaction, sustenance, or rest will follow. Frequenting the holy places, as if by habit but still and always with longing, we become positioned to let the strong words of love in the promised company of Christ reach us, until new direction comes for the week that follows.

*Positioned where the Presence is palpable, let me be warmed
and animated, so I can take flight into adventure and
still know home. Amen*

1 John 4:7–16

Permanence

Psalm 102

My days vanish like smoke.

Poet François Villon, pondering the transience of life, sang for many of us through his question: "But where are the snows of yesteryear?" The writer of the psalm was declarative, but we can convert the statement into a question: "Where is the smoke of yesterday?" Where are any enduring marks of our ancestors, who left few lines that we could recognize except those that mark our own aging faces?

Surrounding all thoughtful prayers is the sense of a need to communicate in the face of the eternal, since time works against us as it did against all who came before us, who loved and built, who destroyed and who regretfully saw destructions, whose tombstones lie toppled.

When we raise funds, hire architects, engage contractors, and build, we like to think that the structure will outlast the mortgage. Let it stand to defy changes in communities and interests, and let it escape the effects of termite and rust. But what we build will not stand. It will not defy the forces that doom every-thing human to the effects of transience.

Thoughts of evanescence that compare our days to smoke that vanishes do get countered by the stronger realization that God's love does not vanish. Unlike smoke, it has substance. Never to be ruined, it will last as long as the love of Christ enwraps and goes before us. Never a monument but always a living Presence, this love forever ignites.

Turn the frail columns of smoke that represent our brief lives
into pillars of fire or stone, to mark divine activity
and offer signals of hope. Amen

Matthew 7:24–27

Help

Psalm 121
I will lift up my eyes to the hills—
from where will my help come?

Old translations in numbers of languages made a sentence out of the question in this verse. It speaks to us about the source of help that is available when we are in trouble, which means any day or every day. Those who once memorized this favored line as a sentence sometimes have difficulty reconceiving it as a query. A dying father, who cherished and often sang the line asked his seminarian son, "Does Hebrew have punctuation?" No. "Then how did they know to change that?" Scholars of language take up such things. The father: "What do scholars know?"

The translators of the psalms can tell from the word order that this is a question, but in the end, to the person seeking solace, it makes little difference. The question answers itself and becomes a statement. Or, as those same scholars believe, another voice—probably that of a priest—answers a questioner and blesses: "Help comes from the Lord, who made heaven and earth," who created its hills and ravines.

These ancient words speak to today, because life remains a walk through valleys where snowslide and avalanche can occur at any moment—during the crossing of a hazardous street; when a dangerous thought crosses the mind; with the opening of an envelope that bears shattering news. Yet from the same "above" that could mean danger comes the help that guides those who welcome it through their walk.

My days, with their narrow passages, are full of danger and confusion, until you as Lord reach down with rescue and help. Amen

Jeremiah 16:19–21

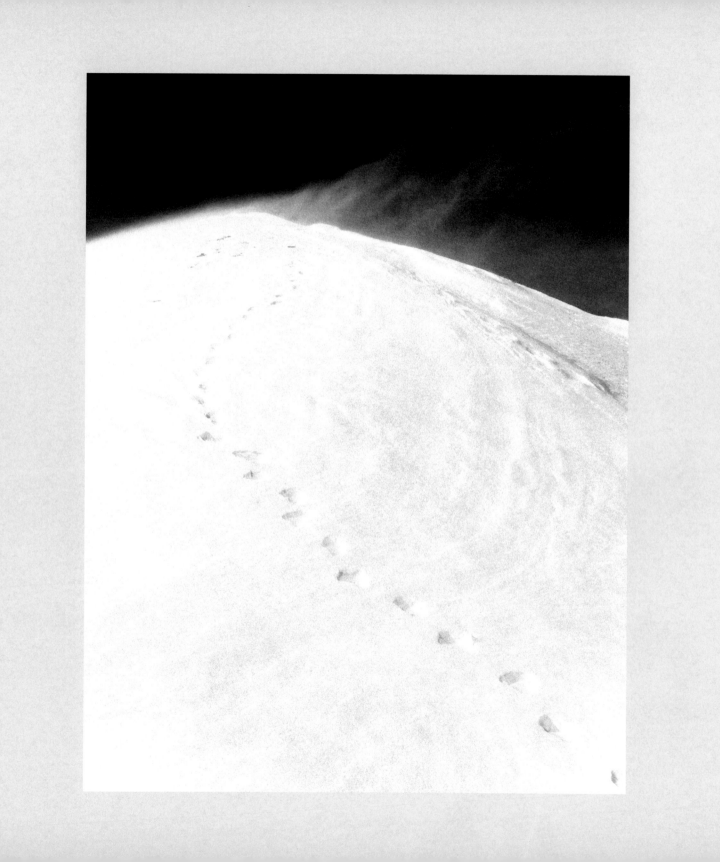

Productivity

Psalm 126
May those who sow in tears reap with shouts of joy.

Seasons are never complete in themselves. Nor does one kind of season—an especially torrid summer, a snow-blasted autumn, a tardy spring—set the terms for all other seasons. Most of us experience cycles of moods, when first barren and then productive periods succeed each other, as in times when nothing seems to be occurring and others when we cannot keep up with the tasks and demands placed on us.

Planters who have just experienced a crop failure due to drought, hail, or flooding sometimes walk away from agriculture and depend henceforth on others for harvests and thus food. But through the ages, most farmers and tillers have been hardy perennials who know to wait for new seasons, fresh opportunities. Their implements are idle, their seeds are stored, their greenhouses await the sun of longer days. But they are ready for their tasks and for whatever is ahead.

In the language of the psalms, there are times when people must "sow in tears," as we do when we sorrow over the past and are reluctant to express hopes too strongly, to plan too fervently. But there is a promise that we shall "reap with shouts of joy." An inventory of most lives provides recall of many such reapings and shouts. We live off them during the fallow seasons, awaiting times for new activity as the God of creation promises to cause the seeds to develop and helps us harvest.

> *We have often sown in tears, seeing disappointments and frustrations;
> give us activities to go with the prospect of reaping in joy. Amen*

Colossians 1:9–20

83

Strength

Psalm 71
Be to me a rock of refuge,
a strong fortress, to save me.

Rocklike northern European castles and fortresses look strong but are cold. Visitors inquire about how dwellers found warmth to go with their strength. A fireplace at best heats a single room; what could it do in great halls and corridors? Guides answer: Chilling as these were in the face of winter winds, fortresses were attractive to the lords and peasants who huddled there when enemies attacked them on the plain.

"Be a strong fortress to save me" is the cry of the heart when the blasts of destruction blow our way. These storms may stir today in the form of questionings, when the basic truths seem unsure. Or some of us will find our ways of work undercut by competitors. If we are to remain responsible, we will also look at the signals in the culture around us, with concern for what they do to overwhelm delicate and cherished value systems. No day passes without some assaults, even if they come in the mildly depressing forms of disappointments. And some of the attacks on faith and hope and love come from within us. We need rescue, help.

"Be a strong fortress to save me" is not a prayer that, when answered, eliminates the cold, at least not all at once. But the One who answers the prayer draws us toward the fire of love and provides for the immediate necessities: strength, security, safety, and salvation. The gusts that bring the snows around us cannot deprive us of divine strength.

> *Rock and Fortress, with the security you provide,*
> *give me a mind and then arms to put new strength to work*
> *for the sake of the powerless. Amen*

2 Samuel 22:1–4

Refreshment

Psalm 42
As a deer longs for flowing streams,
so my soul longs for you, O God.

When the predatory wolf comes into range, the deer begins running through the leafless woods and along the edges of frozen waters. Its body eventually cries out for sustaining water, necessary if it is to continue to elude the attacker and live into spring. Only storytellers and filmmakers "know" what goes on in the inner life of the deer, but they have no difficulty getting us to imagine that by instinct the animal "longs." This is not a being looking for a vintage wine, a new soft drink, a gourmet menu. When all is at risk and resources are sparse, as in winter, the longing is simple. Only water will satisfy.

So it is with the heart of the human, where we do not have to do any imagining to know what "longing" means. Sometimes this longing is induced by panic, when spiritual resources are dry or frozen and we must run to find what was called "living water." More often it takes vague forms and has to compete with other desires and drives, to the point that we may forget the source of that which nourishes.

In these twenty-four hours, when the urgencies of night and the quiet distractions of the day mislead us, we seek and we shall find resources to address what was desperate and move beyond distraction to where God's promises begin to be realized. Through it all, we picture that panting, longing deer finding what it was seeking, and we identify.

When I am thirsty, lead me in your grace to the places where living waters flow, and when I am confused, offer the simpler gifts. Amen

Revelation 7:13–17

Response

Psalm 35:11–28
My prayer came back unanswered.

Familiar are the scenes in which people speak up in bewilderment or rage that their prayers were answered in ways they found unsatisfying. He prayed for something specific, perhaps the survival of a spouse, but God "took her" anyhow. Friends wanted to comfort him, saying that his prayer had indeed been answered. The comfort failed.

Talking about the ways of God to people in such situations is easy compared to dealing with those who storm heaven with their prayers, in season and out of season, but can never become aware of answered prayer, whether of congenial *or* unattractive sorts. After frequent frustrations and perceived failures they announce, in genuine reluctance, that after unanswered prayer went the last traces of faith; life is empty of hope.

The mystery of faith does elude our efforts at diagnosis. Responsibility for unfaith, when someone has been reaching for belief, belongs in the category of "something we have to take up with God, not the psychologists" someday. For now, the thought of the unheard, unanswered prayer is bewildering. It is as if we open hands and hearts and vessels but find them empty. The short term counsel is to emulate the psalmist. He did persist, confident that the Lord would eventually see his servant prosper, until formerly jeering friends would see him do well and "cry continually" in shouts of joy. And we persist.

> *Often I consider prayers to be unheard, unanswered,*
> *only to find responses that come as surprises;*
> *let me look for and find some today. Amen*

Luke 11:1–13

Glory

Psalm 118:24, 26–29
Blessed is the one who comes in the name of the Lord.

Toward the end of winter, when greeting spring, ancient Israel celebrated the Passover, choosing a special time in which to say, "This is the day that the Lord has made." Israel evidently had formal patterns of prayer and greeting, special liturgies outside the house of God, at which words like those were sung. Now Christians also sing the words.

Footnotes in Bibles for Christians include lines pointing out that these psalm lines are "frequently quoted in the New Testament." Gospel-writers connected the figure of the Blessed One with Jesus, who entered Jerusalem on a donkey, before the week leading to his death and triumph. They told of crowds greeting him five days before some killed him.

Forget, for now, that this coming of the Blessed One occurred in the Northern Hemisphere, at a time we can date in spring and thus associate with warming. Picture, for now, that this coming occurs in autumn, as chill comes, as it does to the growing number of millions of Christians in the Southern Hemisphere, or wherever weather is too warm year-round to make much of a difference.

What matters in the psalm, and in the New Testament's use of it, is that Glory is here to be recognized in weakness and humility; that the brightness of divine love breaks into a broken, barren world; that the Blessed One becomes blessed by self-giving love and then blesses us.

As members of crowds long ago came with palms and greetings, let me interrupt my silence and sullen search with a signal of praise. Amen

Luke 19:29–38

Readiness

Psalm 102
My days are like an evening shadow.

The spiritual writer Father John Dunne has observed that great turnings in life, major spiritual awakenings, acts of writing under inspiration, tend to occur when people reach the years around thirty. Before then, death may certainly have come close. A parental death can traumatize the child, and the passing of an adolescent stuns her peers. But to measure one's *own* days toward death is a program that seems remote and artificial to the healthy young. So to observe that life passes quickly, that we are beings-toward-death, that shadows lengthen and that night—*our* night—will fall, sounds like something to save for older people, when actuarial measures work against them. To compare life to evening shadows is natural in life's winter, when night falls earliest.

The psalms we pray are full of shadows for all people of all ages. There is in one psalm a valley of the shadow of death, but in another the praying person also seeks refuge in the shadow of the divine wings. In the present case, the shadowed believer asks that God will not take him or her away "at the mid-point of my life." To think of the brevity of life at mid-point or earlier makes sense just as it does toward the end. Instead of inducing depression or panic, such thought can inspire vocation and readiness for action. Giving voice to prayers that will lead to poise for such activity is the first step toward affirmation.

*Now I would say yes to your bidding and to the calls of others
in need; having measured my days, I would respond. Amen*

Isaiah 40:6–11

Remembrance

Psalm 77:5, 11–20
I consider the days of old,
and remember the years of long ago.

*W*arm memories, old-timers call them. The world of today is brutal and cold, and the future breeds fear. But then, back then, the fire glowed and the family basked in it as the flames from the logs invited everyone to huddle close and tell stories. *Nostalgia,* newer-timers instead call the impulse to revisit days of old. They are suspicious of stories.

Toasty is a way seniors often describe the homes and apartments in which they lived. With their description usually come stories of parental care, of hearty meals around the family table. *Frigid,* say many in a new generation, suspicious of claims that families were once intact and warm; underneath the illusions of warmth, cold must have reigned.

How things were in the past and how they get remembered depends on the highly diverse experiences of very different people who lived then or who make up stories about long ago. Only one constant appears through all the rememberings and tellings: the Lord of times and places was present then and is now. This is the Lord of remembrance.

While revisiting the past today may call up stories of hardship as well as plenty, of abuse along with affirmations, one aspect of recall helps believers endure today. This is the awareness that hidden in the past and revealed during response to it is the God of long ago—and of seasons ahead—the God who cared and cares.

Be a presence and visit us in the world of clocks set for today and calendars ready to be torn for tomorrow; be a loving presence. Amen

Hebrews 1:1–4

Guidance

Psalm 37
Though we stumble, we shall not fall headlong.

F"alling," a poem by James Dickey, puts the reader into the mind of a flight attendant who fell more than 30,000 feet to the Kansas soil when an airplane door opened unexpectedly. The horror of the headlong drop, where there is no chance of recovering a foothold, grips the reader who thus falls at second hand. But falling occurs also on the level ground, in ordinary life, as when pioneers stumbled during a blizzard or when travelers leave their marooned autos along the drift-full highway.

Avoiding the manifest dangers of the winter landscape will help minimize the dangers of falling, but still we stumble. We know that misfortune is unavoidable through the years. In any case, averting the headlong fall can lead to self-assurance and then stumbling: "I, for one, will go alone through life without missteps." Again, however, "I" will not. Morally a person may avoid criminal activity and yet be nagged by petty impulses. Spiritually one may not fall into total skepticism and yet be harassed by doubts. Intellectually one may not fall into nihilism, but still unanswered questions can be plaguing, almost paralyzing.

Faith says, as does the psalm, that what keeps us from headlong plunges is the fact the "the Lord holds us by the hand." Confidence in that guiding hand aids us through the wintry and drifting passages of our souls until we come to more secure footing again.

As a stumbler I have come to know: it is your hand that rights and guides me, giving strength. I seek that hand today. Amen

Isaiah 58:9–12

Salvation

Psalm 116
I will lift up the cup of salvation.

When the winter wanderer located a way to the pilgrim hostel, nothing to be found was more cheering than the greeting that came with the cup of warm mead. The fallen victim of war on barren battlefields finds no help more enlivening than the cup of water. The patient rings the bell and a nurse comes with a cup to quench the thirst and help restore health. In all three cases, the assuaging was momentary, though satisfying.

Satisfying and lasting was the the cup of salvation lifted by a psalmist in Israel, after his healing. And in the New Covenant story, on the night before he died, Jesus also lifted the cup of salvation and imparted it to those near him, promising to do so again in the regathering at a feast to come. Twenty centuries later, many celebrants around the cup sing of it as the cup of salvation.

The Gospels say that on the night of his Last Supper, Jesus prayed that another cup, a cup of suffering, would be removed. It was not, and he was to take what it contained, following to the cross of divine love.

So it is that the cup of suffering and the cup of salvation, the crown of thorns and the glorious crown worn by the world's healer, fuse into one in the imaging of those who follow today. *Salvation* back then meant "healing" and "saving." To the believing heart, it still does.

> *When the cup of salvation is lifted, let this thirsty one drink; let this needy one be saved, rescued, made whole, and set in company. Amen*

Matthew 26:26–29

Identification

Psalm 22
My God, my God, why have you forsaken me?

Jesus came, says a hymn, "in midst of coldest winter," though no one knows assuredly, or at all, in which season he was born. He was put to death in the moderate springtime Passover season. But no event other than this dying on a cross better matches the negatives of a wintry spirit in the heart. The death of Christ signals lethal Arctic Circle-style cold, where winds blow, where in minutes any abandoned person would die.

Jesus was coldly abandoned on the cross, when he was effecting what divine and perfect love alone could do, through suffering, into death. That according to the Gospels he *was* abandoned is clear from the words of a psalm we hear from his lips: "My God, my God, why have you forsaken me?" Not "could you?" or "will you?" or "might you?" abandon me, but why *did* his God leave him to hang there alone?

That Jesus had rapport with God is clear from almost all pages of the Gospels. This day, after he asked that the cup of suffering be passed by him—it was not—he could not for the moment feel God's nearness. The tundra winds of the soul, the barren landscape of the heart, the devastation of the spirit: all these were capsuled in the chill crucifying cry, "My God, my God, why have you forsaken me?"

In faith, the abandoned Christ is raised by God and is again identified with God. No one identified with Christ ever has to be abandoned.

Let me live in awareness that in living and in dying I will never be forsaken, that you will be company in all I experience. Amen

Matthew 27:38–50

Vigil

Psalm 77
In the night my hand is stretched out without wearying.

Perhaps we have not done enough, on these pages and through the days of this pilgrimage, to deal with the terrors of night—wintry night—in the soul. In the day, sunshine and shadow may make their appearance, while paths and landmarks are visible, hiding places are exposed, and time is endurable. But at night, in the spirit's snow and wind, the landmarks disappear and the moorings are not to be found.

Perhaps on this pilgrimage we have not spent as much time as we should on the lines that we do *not* quote from the psalms we are reading. They often reinforce the texts. Thus in this case the setting has one praying at night, "crying" and "seeking," "moaning" until "my spirit faints." The same lines, however, also supply the first words of strength and comfort that have meant and mean so much to us as we experience not the killing but the promise of winter.

So, here: the one who prays calls to mind the wonderful acts and deeds of God. The two darkest nights in history, from believers' points of view, were a Friday and Saturday when Jesus was entombed in a hole in Jerusalem. In the acts and deeds on a third day, God is to raise him. But for now there is only the vigil of quiet, silence, waiting, until new life is to come. For now, the act of seeking through the night with hands outstretched unwearyingly is the most productive mark of hope.

> *Visit me in the daylight hours and through the longer night,*
> *as expectation grows for the end of vigil and the arrival of*
> *new life. Amen*

Micah 7:7–10a

Risen Life

Psalm 118
I shall not die;
I shall live.

Scholars note that the Hebrew Scriptures have very few clear references to a fulfilled life with God beyond the grave. Christians now, however, connect their own resurrection with that of Jesus, a rising to life that is described not as an ordinary act, not even an ordinary "resurrection." Instead, what happened in and to the risen Jesus is pictured as something without analogy or comparison. It is something wholly new. He is the first fruit of the new creation.

Today stained-glass images, trumpets, the company of fellow believers, and clear readings of Scripture all work to reinforce the faith of those who believe that their new life comes with Christ's. But on the unending pilgrimage of faith and hope, the resurrection experience is not confined to one day, one story, one mood. It occurs every morning, on every day called the Lord's Day, and upon every act of turning from old to new, of accepting the new life that brings its own graces.

For all that we have gained from this walk through the figurative winter of the spirit as a time of promise, we are sustained in new ways when the imaged angle of the sun changes, to warm the heart. What was fallow now springs to life. What was frozen now flows. What looked like death is replaced by life. The warming Son is here, and now it is easy to adopt old psalm language: I shall not die; I shall live.

> *Let every day be a festival of the resurrection, as I walk forward*
> *with a spring in the step and spring in the heart:*
> *hope realized in part. Amen*

Romans 6:3–11

The Photographs

Winter changes everything outdoors, including photography. The snowy landscape presents a wide variety of opportunities and challenges for both camera and photographer.

All of the photographs in this book were made in the northern United States, usually in snow depths of two to three feet. In such conditions, mobility is the most obvious challenge; snowshoes provide the solution. Almost none of the scenes depicted here would have been accessible without them. Of course, with the snowshoe-shod photographer standing on top of the snow and the tripod-mounted camera brought up to eye level, the tripod legs must extend two to three feet longer than normal to reach solid ground. (A tripod is important in any season, not merely to steady the camera for sharper pictures but because mounting the camera in a fixed position allows more thoughtful and precise composition of the photograph.)

The further north one goes in winter, the less the time between sunrise and sunset. In mid-winter the amount of daylight available for photographing is little more than half as long as it is in June. Combined with less-than-pleasant temperatures, these shortened days encourage efficient time-management techniques on the part of the photographer. The low winter sun also greatly affects the quality of light, particularly with respect to shadows. Very long shadows—for much of the day, longer than the object itself (see, for example, pages 6 and 45)—require greater attention to shadow "management," lest crisscrossing shadows from various objects result in a confusing jumble of gray lines.

Landscape photographers learn early on that to photograph a scene well, it is often best to walk through it and around it to find the best view. This principle, however, must be modified a bit in winter, because such scouting will leave obvious tracks and a single errant snowshoe-print can ruin a picture. Every potentially photographable scene must be approached cautiously to avoid stomping through an area that in a few minutes one wishes were an unscathed background (at which point there is no recourse except to move on—or wait for fresh snowfall!). Similarly, a scene can be ruined by any marks made on the snow since the last snowfall, whether from other people, animals (in deep snow their tracks look more like creature-sized trenches than paw prints!), or fallen twigs. The sooner one photographs after a new snow, the better one's chances of finding pristine nature scenes.

The Photographs

Snow and ice are often surprisingly delicate (see, for example, pages 37 and 65). Icicles and ice formations can shatter like a dropped vase without any warning at all (sometimes while the photographer is readying the camera!), and snow configurations that look random and happenstance lose their visual allure upon human contact. Touching, bumping, or breathing on a close-up snow scene ruins it immediately. Even on the coldest days, the warmth of the new morning can alter a snowscape rapidly; the time between the direct morning sun making the frost glisten (page 105) and the frost beginning to slip away is measured in seconds, not minutes.

Snow is usually accompanied by temperatures low enough to quickly fog lenses, freeze condensation inside the camera, and exhaust batteries, so the photographer must be constantly alert to the effect of cold weather on equipment. Care has to be taken when moving cameras, lenses, and film between warm and cold environments (inside and outside), and if a camera does not offer fully mechanical operation, the batteries have to be kept warm—even during use—to prevent premature failure. In the harshest conditions a basic mechanical camera is often a better choice than the latest full-featured electronic one. For cameras that automatically wind film very quickly, the dry winter air can cause static electricity inside the camera, leaving lightninglike marks on the film. In extremely cold temperatures, film can become brittle and even crack.

Attention also must be paid to keeping warm the most important link in the photographing process: the photographer. Personal protection against the elements is as critical as equipment selection, not only for safety but for comfort. Proper clothing allows ample time to explore possible scenes and to carefully set up and compose photographs. Modern fabrics combined with old-fashioned common sense can reduce to a minimum dangerous or limiting situations.

Basically, however, there are no difficult "tricks" to winter photography, other than to pare down as much as possible the equipment choice to what works. The photographer's introduction discusses how "winter clarifies." Taking pictures in cold weather acutely clarifies a key rule in photography, as well: the simpler the equipment, the fewer the problems.

The Photographs

Technical Notes

Several medium-format cameras were used to make these photographs, all using 120 roll film. (With negative sizes of 6x7 and 6x9 cm—more than four times larger than a 35mm negative—less enlargement is necessary to achieve a normal-sized print.) The cameras were always mounted on a tripod, not handheld. Black-and-white ISO 100 film was used, and the prints were handmade by the photographer using traditional darkroom techniques.

Acknowledgments

Coordinating the production of books like those in this series is a major endeavor. To meld the photographs and words requires the skills of an editor, a planner, a producer, a manager, a print coordinator, and a communicator— someone who understands both theology and esthetics. We gratefully acknowledge that once again Ann Rehfeldt of Sterling Images has filled all of these roles quietly and effectively. All who read this book will profit from her labors.

Because most readers who look at books of photographs do not have opportunity to see the original prints, the reproduction quality of each image is crucial to its effectiveness. It has been a privilege to work again with the best in the business, Gardner Lithograph, the company that has printed the work of America's greatest photographers (including the popular Ansel Adams calendars, posters, and books). Special thanks are owed to David Gray Gardner and to Kevin Broady, John Visone, and Robert Sweet, each of whom played a key role in ensuring the quality of the reproductions.